The Atlantis Dialogue
The Original Story of the Lost City, Civilization, Continent, and Empire
— Plato —

The legend of Atlantis—you've heard about it, read about it, seen it in videos, shows, and movies. Now go straight to the source!

Atlantis was first introduced by the Greek philosopher Plato in two "dialogues" he wrote in the fourth century B.C. His tale of a great empire that sank beneath the waves has generated countless books, dramatic adaptations, archeological expeditions, and more.

It has also sparked thousands of years of debate and speculation. Did Plato mean his tale as ancient history, or just as a parable to help illustrate his philosophy? Why did he break it off in the middle, never completing our only primary account of this "lost" civilization? And why did Aristotle, Plato's student, once say of Atlantis, "He who invented it also destroyed it."

In *The Atlantis Dialogue*, you'll find everything Plato wrote about Atlantis, in the context he intended. Now you can read it and judge for yourself!

"The perfect reference for that lost civilization . . . Accurate, concise, and understandable. Anyone who is a fan or student of Atlantis should, no, *must* have this book in their library."

> Sharon D. Anderson, author,
> *Atlantis: The Final Days*

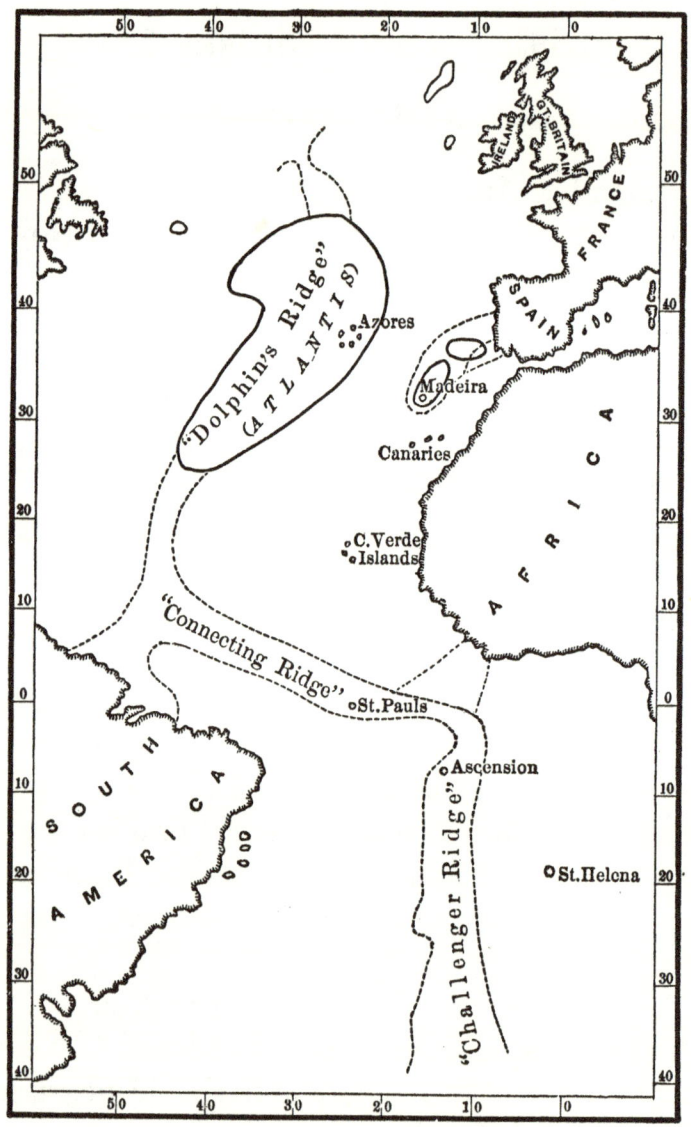

Map of Atlantis from Ignatius Donnelly, 1882

The Atlantis Dialogue

The Original Story of the Lost City, Civilization, Continent, and Empire

Plato

Edited with an Introduction by
Aaron Shepard

Translated by B. Jowett

Shepard Publications
Bellingham, Washington

Introduction, compilation copyright © 2001, 2017, 2023, 2024 by Aaron Shepard

The text of this dialogue consists of extracts from the *Timaeus* and the *Critias* in *The Dialogues of Plato,* third edition, translated by B. Jowett, Oxford University Press, 1892, volume 2.

Cover: Map of Atlantis from *Mundus Subterreanus,* by Athanasius Kircher, 1664. (North is at bottom.)

Frontispiece: Map of Atlantis from *Atlantis: The Antediluvian World*, by Ignatius Donnelly, 1882. (Original caption: "Map of Atlantis, with its islands and connecting ridges, from deep-sea soundings.")

Library of Congress subject headings:
Atlantis
Plato—Timaeus—English
Plato—Critias—English

Version 2.1

Contents

Introduction, by Aaron Shepard   5

THE ATLANTIS DIALOGUE   11

Recommended Reading   63

Introduction

Atlantis was first introduced to world literature by the Greek philosopher Plato in two "dialogues" he wrote in the city-state of Athens in the fourth century B.C. As a literary form, a dialogue is a cross between an essay and a short story—it discusses serious ideas, but by means of a fictional conversation. The main character in Plato's dialogues is his mentor Socrates, though all words and speeches are Plato's own. (When Socrates heard Plato publicly read one of his first dialogues, he declared, "By Heracles, what a lot of lies this young man is telling about me!")

The dialogues in which Atlantis appears are the *Timaeus* and the *Critias*. These were apparently meant as the first two in a connected series of three, but Plato never finished it. In fact, the *Critias* itself—the dialogue in which the bulk of the story of Atlantis was to be told—breaks off in mid-paragraph, leaving us only a fragment.

The premise of the existing two dialogues is that Socrates has entertained several guests the day before with his concept of an ideal society. (This militarist utopia of Plato's is discussed fully in his earlier dialogue, the *Republic*.) But Socrates was discontent, feeling that the principles he offered should be fleshed out by a story of how such a society would show its merit, especially in an event of war. So he charged his guests to come up with such a tale.

In response, his guest Critias—in real life, an older relative of Plato—has now dredged up a childhood memory of a history passed down in his family from Solon, a legendary lawgiver of Athens. Solon himself heard it from priests he met while visiting Egypt, who revealed to him what no Athenian knew: That the history of Athens went back nine thousand years, to a time when its society was based on exactly the utopian principles that Socrates propounded! (One can almost see Plato winking at the reader.)

The priests told Solon how the warriors of this ancient Athens single-handedly turned back an invasion of Europe by the greatest power the world had known—the island empire of Atlantis. And finally, how both Atlantis and ancient Athens were destroyed by a cataclysmic earthquake.

With Socrates's approval, his three guests are now to tell him the full story of this war, each relating his part in turn. Oddly, Timaeus's part—which takes up the remaining bulk of the first dialogue—is not really part of the story at all, but an extended prologue in which Plato discusses the creation and nature of the universe.

It is when Critias's turn comes, in the second dialogue, that the story begins in earnest. Critias describes first ancient Athens, then the history, geography, and society of Atlantis. But just as he starts on the events leading to the war, Plato abandons the project.

Why didn't Plato finish it? Many possibilities can be imagined. Perhaps he meant to come back to it but never got the chance. Perhaps he worried that Atlantis might seem more appealing than his idealized Athens. Perhaps his thoughts echoed those he gave Socrates, who declares himself incapable of relating such a story. Or perhaps he simply felt he had better things to write.

Whatever Plato's reason, it is ironic that this unfinished tale of Atlantis has become his most celebrated offering, known even to those who know nothing of Plato himself. He has indeed fashioned an enduring and alluring myth, engaging and inspiring through the centuries.

Curiously, this myth has taken on its most fervent life only in modern times. Starting in the late 1800s, literally thousands of books have discussed whether Atlantis really existed. It should be clear, though, from reading Plato's story in context that Atlantis was an invention designed to help illustrate his philosophy. Such creations were common in the writings of both Plato and his contemporaries. In light of this, most of those contemporaries either withheld judgment on the truth of Plato's tale or assumed it to be allegory. Plato's own student Aristotle remarked on the Atlantis of his teacher, "He who invented it also destroyed it."

How then did the existence of Atlantis become such a popular notion? That is an entire story in itself, perhaps best covered by L. Sprague de Camp in his intellectual history *Lost Continents* (Dover, New York, 1970). De Camp's book should be read by anyone curious how a wrongheaded idea can grow and spread until it is impossible to root out.

The Atlantis Dialogue—as I've titled this volume—was compiled by attaching the beginning of the *Timaeus* to all but the introduction of the *Critias*. (A divider in the text marks the borderline.) The result is a compact and unified work that presents everything Plato said about Atlantis, and in the context he intended. The translation is by Benjamin Jowett from his collection *The Dialogues of Plato,* third edition (Oxford University Press, 1892), for long the standard in the field. To compare a more recent effort, you might wish to see *Timaeus and Critias,* translated by Desmond Lee (Penguin, London, 1977).

Aaron Shepard

Aaron Shepard specializes in retelling classic world literature and folklore. He can be found online at www.aaronshep.com.

The Atlantis Dialogue

Socrates. One, two, three; but where, my dear Timaeus, is the fourth of those who were yesterday my guests and are to be my entertainers today?

Timaeus. He has been taken ill, Socrates; for he would not willingly have been absent from this gathering.

Socrates. Then, if he is not coming, you and the two others must supply his place.

Timaeus. Certainly, and we will do all that we can; having been handsomely entertained by you yesterday, those of us who remain should be only too glad to return your hospitality.

Socrates. Do you remember what were the points of which I required you to speak?

Timaeus. We remember some of them, and you will be here to remind us of anything which we have forgotten—or rather, if we are not troubling you, will you briefly recapitulate the whole, and then the particulars will be more firmly fixed in our memories?

Socrates. To be sure I will: The chief theme of my yesterday's discourse was the State—how constituted and of what citizens composed it would seem likely to be most perfect.

Timaeus. Yes, Socrates; and what you said of it was very much to our mind.

Socrates. Did we not begin by separating the husbandmen and the artisans from the class of defenders of the State?

Timaeus. Yes.

Socrates. And when we had given to each one that single employment and particular art which was suited to his nature, we spoke of those who were intended to be our warriors, and said that they were to be guardians of the city against attacks from within as well as from without, and to have no other employment; they were to be merciful in judging their subjects, of whom they were by nature friends, but fierce to their enemies, when they came across them in battle.

Timaeus. Exactly.

Socrates. We said, if I am not mistaken, that the guardians should be gifted with a temperament in a high degree both passionate and philosophical; and that then they would be as they ought to be, gentle to their friends and fierce with their enemies.

Timaeus. Certainly.

Socrates. And what did we say of their education? Were they not to be trained in gymnastic, and music, and all other sorts of knowledge which were proper for them?

Timaeus. Very true.

Socrates. And being thus trained they were not to consider gold or silver or anything else to be their own private property; they were to be like hired troops, receiving pay for keeping guard from those who were protected by them—the pay was to be no more than would suffice for men of simple life; and they were to spend in common, and to live together in the continual practice of virtue, which was to be their sole pursuit.

Timaeus. That was also said.

Socrates. Neither did we forget the women; of whom we declared, that their natures should be assimilated and brought into harmony with those of the men, and that common pursuits should be assigned to them both in time of war and in their ordinary life.

Timaeus. That, again, was as you say.

Socrates. And what about the procreation of children? Or rather was not the proposal too singular to be forgotten? For all wives and children were to be in common, to the intent that no one should ever know his own child, but they were to imagine that they were all one family; those who were within a suitable limit of age were to be brothers and sisters, those who were of an elder generation parents and grandparents, and those of a younger, children and grandchildren.

Timaeus. Yes, and the proposal is easy to remember, as you say.

Socrates. And do you also remember how, with a view of securing as far as we could the best breed, we said that the chief magistrates, male and female, should contrive secretly, by the use of certain lots, so to arrange the nuptial meeting, that the bad of either sex and the good of either sex might pair with their like; and there was to be no quarrelling on this account, for they would imagine that the union was a mere accident, and was to be attributed to the lot?

Timaeus. I remember.

Socrates. And you remember how we said that the children of the good parents were to be educated, and the children of the bad secretly dispersed among the inferior citizens; and while they were all growing up the rulers were to be on the lookout, and to bring up from below in their turn those who were worthy, and those among themselves who were unworthy were to take the places of those who came up?

Timaeus. True.

Socrates. Then have I now given you all the heads of our yesterday's discussion? Or is there anything more, my dear Timaeus, which has been omitted?

Timaeus. Nothing, Socrates; it was just as you have said.

Socrates. I should like, before proceeding further, to tell you how I feel about the State which we have described. I might compare myself to a person who, on beholding beautiful animals either created by the painter's art, or, better still, alive but at rest, is seized with a desire of seeing them in motion or engaged in some struggle or conflict to which their forms appear suited; this is my feeling about the State which we have been describing. There are conflicts which all cities undergo, and I should like to hear someone tell of our own city carrying on a struggle against her neighbours, and how she went out to war in a becoming manner, and when at war showed by the greatness of her actions and the magnanimity of her words in dealing with other cities a result worthy of her training and education.

Now I, Critias and Hermocrates, am conscious that I myself should never be able to celebrate the city and her citizens in a befitting manner, and I am not surprised at my own incapacity; to me the wonder is rather that the poets, present as well as past, are no better—not that I mean to depreciate them; but everyone can see that they are a tribe of imitators, and will imitate best and most easily the life in which they have been brought up; while that which is beyond the range of a man's education he finds hard to carry out in action, and still harder adequately to represent in language. I am aware that the Sophists have plenty of brave words and fair conceits, but I am afraid that being only wanderers from one city to another, and having never had habitations of their own, they may fail in their conception of philosophers and statesmen, and may not know what they do and say in time of war, when they are fighting or holding parley with their enemies.

And thus people of your class are the only ones remaining who are fitted by nature and education to take part at once both in politics and philosophy. Here is Timaeus, of Locris in Italy, a city which has admirable laws, and who is himself in wealth and rank the equal of any of his fellow citizens; he has held the most important and honourable offices in his own state, and, as I believe, has scaled the heights of all philosophy; and here is Critias, whom every Athenian knows to be no novice in the matters of which we are speaking; and as to Hermocrates, I am assured by many witnesses that his genius and education qualify him to take part in any speculation of the kind. And therefore yesterday when I saw that you wanted me to describe the formation of the State, I readily assented, being very well aware, that if you only would, none were better qualified to carry the discussion further, and that when you had engaged our city in a suitable war, you of all men living could best exhibit her playing a fitting part. When I had completed my task, I in return imposed this other task upon you. You conferred together and agreed to entertain me today, as I had entertained you, with a feast of discourse. Here am I in festive array, and no man can be more ready for the promised banquet.

Hermocrates. And we too, Socrates, as Timaeus says, will not be wanting in enthusiasm; and there is no excuse for not complying with your request. As soon as we arrived yesterday at the guest chamber of Critias, with whom we are staying, or rather on our way thither, we talked the matter over, and he told us an ancient tradition, which I wish, Critias, that you would repeat to Socrates, so that he may help us to judge whether it will satisfy his requirements or not.

Critias. I will, if Timaeus, who is our other partner, approves.

Timaeus. I quite approve.

Critias. Then listen, Socrates, to a tale which, though strange, is certainly true, having been attested by Solon, who was the wisest of the seven sages. He was a relative and a dear friend of my great-grandfather, Dropides, as he himself says in many passages of his poems; and he told the story to Critias, my grandfather, who remembered and repeated it to us. There were of old, he said, great and marvellous actions of the Athenian city, which have passed into oblivion through lapse of time and the destruction of mankind, and one in particular, greater than all the rest. This we will now rehearse. It will be a fitting monument of our gratitude to you, and a hymn of praise true and worthy of the goddess, on this her day of festival.

Socrates. Very good. And what is this ancient famous action of the Athenians, which Critias declared, on the authority of Solon, to be not a mere legend, but an actual fact?

Critias. I will tell an old-world story which I heard from an aged man; for Critias, at the time of telling it, was as he said nearly ninety years of age, and I was about ten. Now the day was that day of the Apaturia which is called the Registration of Youth, at which, according to custom, our parents gave prizes for recitations, and the poems of several poets were recited by us boys, and many of us sang the poems of Solon, which at that time had not gone out of fashion. One of our tribe, either because he thought so or to please Critias, said that in his judgment Solon was not only the wisest of men, but also the noblest of poets. The old man, as I very well remember, brightened up at hearing this and said, smiling: Yes, Amynander, if Solon had only, like other poets, made poetry the business of his life, and had completed the tale which he brought with him from Egypt, and had not been compelled, by reason of the factions and troubles which he found stirring in his own country when he came home, to attend to other matters, in my opinion he would have been as famous as Homer or Hesiod, or any poet.

And what was the tale about, Critias? said Amynander.

About the greatest action which the Athenians ever did, and which ought to have been the most famous, but, through the lapse of time and the destruction of the actors, it has not come down to us.

Tell us, said the other, the whole story, and how and from whom Solon heard this veritable tradition.

He replied: In the Egyptian Delta, at the head of which the river Nile divides, there is a certain district which is called the district of Sais, and the great city of the district is also called Sais, and is the city from which King Amasis came. The citizens have a deity for their foundress; she is called in the Egyptian tongue Neith, and is asserted by them to be the same whom the Hellenes call Athene; they are great lovers of the Athenians, and say that they are in some way related to them. To this city came Solon, and was received there with great honour; he asked the priests, who were most skilful in such matters, about antiquity, and made the discovery that neither he nor any other Hellene knew anything worth mentioning about the times of old.

On one occasion, wishing to draw them on to speak of antiquity, he began to tell about the most ancient things in our part of the world—about Phoroneus, who is called 'the first man,' and about Niobe; and after the Deluge, of the survival of Deucalion and Pyrrha; and he traced the genealogy of their descendants, and reckoning up the dates, tried to compute how many years ago the events of which he was speaking happened. Thereupon one of the priests, who was of a very great age, said: O Solon, Solon, you Hellenes are never anything but children, and there is not an old man among you. Solon in return asked him what he meant. I mean to say, he replied, that in mind you are all young; there is no old opinion handed down among you by ancient tradition, nor any science which is hoary with age. And I will tell you why. There have been, and will be again, many destructions of mankind arising out of many causes; the greatest have been brought about by the agencies of fire and water, and other lesser ones by innumerable other causes.

There is a story, which even you have preserved, that once upon a time Phaëthon, the son of Helios, having yoked the steeds in his father's chariot, because he was not able to drive them in the path of his father, burnt up all that was upon the earth, and was himself destroyed by a thunderbolt. Now this has the form of a myth, but really signifies a declination of the bodies moving in the heavens around the earth, and a great conflagration of things upon the earth, which recurs after long intervals; at such times those who live upon the mountains and in dry and lofty places are more liable to destruction than those who dwell by rivers or on the seashore. And from this calamity the Nile, who is our never-failing saviour, delivers and preserves us. When, on the other hand, the gods purge the earth with a deluge of water, the survivors in your country are herdsmen and shepherds who dwell on the mountains, but those who, like you, live in cities are carried by the rivers into the sea. Whereas in this land, neither then nor at any other time, does the water come down from above on the fields, having always a tendency to come up from below; for which reason the traditions preserved here are the most ancient.

The fact is, that wherever the extremity of winter frost or of summer sun does not prevent, mankind exists, sometimes in greater, sometimes in lesser numbers. And whatever happened either in your country or in ours, or in any other region of which we are informed—if there were any actions noble or great or in any other way remarkable, they have all been written down by us of old, and are preserved in our temples. Whereas just when you and other nations are beginning to be provided with letters and the other requisites of civilized life, after the usual interval, the stream from heaven, like a pestilence, comes pouring down, and leaves only those of you who are destitute of letters and education; and so you have to begin all over again like children, and know nothing of what happened in ancient times, either among us or among yourselves.

As for those genealogies of yours which you just now recounted to us, Solon, they are no better than the tales of children. In the first place you remember a single deluge only, but there were many previous ones; in the next place, you do not know that there formerly dwelt in your land the fairest and noblest race of men which ever lived, and that you and your whole city are descended from a small seed or remnant of them which survived. And this was unknown to you, because, for many generations, the survivors of that destruction died, leaving no written word. For there was a time, Solon, before the great deluge of all, when the city which now is Athens was first in war and in every way the best governed of all cities, and is said to have performed the noblest deeds and to have had the fairest constitution of any of which tradition tells, under the face of heaven.

Solon marvelled at his words, and earnestly requested the priests to inform him exactly and in order about these former citizens. You are welcome to hear about them, Solon, said the priest, both for your own sake and for that of your city, and above all, for the sake of the goddess who is the common patron and parent and educator of both our cities. She founded your city a thousand years before ours, receiving from the Earth and Hephaestus the seed of your race, and afterwards she founded ours, of which the constitution is recorded in our sacred registers to be eight thousand years old. As touching your citizens of nine thousand years ago, I will briefly inform you of their laws and of their most famous action; the exact particulars of the whole we will hereafter go through at our leisure in the sacred registers themselves.

If you compare these very laws with ours you will find that many of ours are the counterpart of yours as they were in the olden time. In the first place, there is the caste of priests, which is separated from all the others; next, there are the artificers, who ply their several crafts by themselves and do not intermix; and also there is the class of shepherds and of hunters, as well as that of husbandmen; and you will observe, too, that the warriors in Egypt are distinct from all the other classes, and are commanded by the law to devote themselves solely to military pursuits; moreover, the weapons which they carry are shields and spears, a style of equipment which the goddess taught of Asiatics first to us, as in your part of the world first to you. Then as to wisdom, do you observe how our law from the very first made a study of the whole order of things, extending even to prophecy and medicine which gives health, out of these divine elements deriving what was needful for human life, and adding every sort of knowledge which was akin to them.

All this order and arrangement the goddess first imparted to you when establishing your city; and she chose the spot of earth in which you were born, because she saw that the happy temperament of the seasons in that land would produce the wisest of men. Wherefore the goddess, who was a lover both of war and of wisdom, selected and first of all settled that spot which was the most likely to produce men most like herself. And there you dwelt, having such laws as these and still better ones, and excelled all mankind in all virtue, as became the children and disciples of the gods.

Many great and wonderful deeds are recorded of your state in our histories. But one of them exceeds all the rest in greatness and valour. For these histories tell of a mighty power which unprovoked made an expedition against the whole of Europe and Asia, and to which your city put an end. This power came forth out of the Atlantic Ocean, for in those days the Atlantic was navigable; and there was an island situated in front of the straits which are by you called the pillars of Heracles; the island was larger than Libya and Asia put together, and was the way to other islands, and from these you might pass to the whole of the opposite continent which surrounded the true ocean; for this sea which is within the Straits of Heracles is only a harbour, having a narrow entrance, but that other is a real sea, and the surrounding land may be most truly called a boundless continent.

Now in this island of Atlantis there was a great and wonderful empire which had rule over the whole island and several others, and over parts of the continent, and, furthermore, the men of Atlantis had subjected the parts of Libya within the columns of Heracles as far as Egypt, and of Europe as far as Tyrrhenia. This vast power, gathered into one, endeavoured to subdue at a blow our country and yours and the whole of the region within the straits; and then, Solon, your country shone forth, in the excellence of her virtue and strength, among all mankind. She was preeminent in courage and military skill, and was the leader of the Hellenes. And when the rest fell off from her, being compelled to stand alone, after having undergone the very extremity of danger, she defeated and triumphed over the invaders, and preserved from slavery those who were not yet subjugated, and generously liberated all the rest of us who dwell within the pillars. But afterwards there occurred violent earthquakes and floods; and in a single day and night of misfortune all your warlike men in a body sank into the earth, and the island of Atlantis in like manner disappeared in the depths of the sea. For which reason the sea in those parts is impassable and impenetrable, because there is a shoal of mud in the way; and this was caused by the subsidence of the island.

I have told you briefly, Socrates, what the aged Critias heard from Solon and related to us. And when you were speaking yesterday about your city and citizens, the tale which I have just been repeating to you came into my mind, and I remarked with astonishment how, by some mysterious coincidence, you agreed in almost every particular with the narrative of Solon; but I did not like to speak at the moment. For a long time had elapsed, and I had forgotten too much; I thought that I must first of all run over the narrative in my own mind, and then I would speak. And so I readily assented to your request yesterday, considering that in all such cases the chief difficulty is to find a tale suitable to our purpose, and that with such a tale we should be fairly well provided.

And therefore, as Hermocrates has told you, on my way home yesterday I at once communicated the tale to my companions as I remembered it; and after I left them, during the night by thinking I recovered nearly the whole of it. Truly, as is often said, the lessons of our childhood make a wonderful impression on our memories; for I am not sure that I could remember all the discourse of yesterday, but I should be much surprised if I forgot any of these things which I have heard very long ago. I listened at the time with child-like interest to the old man's narrative; he was very ready to teach me, and I asked him again and again to repeat his words, so that like an indelible picture they were branded into my mind. As soon as the day broke, I rehearsed them, as he spoke them, to my companions, that they, as well as myself, might have something to say.

And now, Socrates, to make an end of my preface, I am ready to tell you the whole tale. I will give you not only the general heads, but the particulars, as they were told to me. The city and citizens, which you yesterday described to us in fiction, we will now transfer to the world of reality. It shall be the ancient city of Athens, and we will suppose that the citizens whom you imagined, were our veritable ancestors, of whom the priest spoke; they will perfectly harmonize, and there will be no inconsistency in saying that the citizens of your republic are these ancient Athenians. Let us divide the subject among us, and all endeavour according to our ability gracefully to execute the task which you have imposed upon us. Consider then,

Socrates, if this narrative is suited to the purpose, or whether we should seek for some other instead.

Socrates. And what other, Critias, can we find that will be better than this, which is natural and suitable to the festival of the goddess, and has the very great advantage of being a fact and not a fiction? How or where shall we find another if we abandon this? We cannot, and therefore you must tell the tale, and good luck to you; and I in return for my yesterday's discourse will now rest and be a listener.

* * *

Critias. Let me begin by observing first of all, that nine thousand was the sum of years which had elapsed since the war which was said to have taken place between those who dwelt outside the pillars of Heracles and all who dwelt within them; this war I am going to describe. Of the combatants on the one side, the city of Athens was reported to have been the leader and to have fought out the war; the combatants on the other side were commanded by the kings of Atlantis, which, as I was saying, was an island greater in extent than Libya and Asia, and when afterwards sunk by an earthquake, became an impassable barrier of mud to voyagers sailing from hence to any part of the ocean. The progress of the history will unfold the various nations of barbarians and families of Hellenes which then existed, as they successively appear on the scene; but I must describe first of all Athenians of that day, and their enemies who fought with them, and then the respective powers and governments of the two kingdoms. Let us give the precedence to Athens.

In the days of old the gods had the whole earth distributed among them by allotment. There was no quarrelling; for you cannot rightly suppose that the gods did not know what was proper for each of them to have, or, knowing this, that they would seek to procure for themselves by contention that which more properly belonged to others. They all of them by just apportionment obtained what they wanted, and peopled their own districts; and when they had peopled them they tended us, their nurselings and possessions, as shepherds tend their flocks, excepting only that they did not use blows or bodily force, as shepherds do, but governed us like pilots from the stern of the vessel, which is an easy way of guiding animals, holding our souls by the rudder of persuasion according to their own pleasure—thus did they guide all mortal creatures.

Now different gods had their allotments in different places which they set in order. Hephaestus and Athene, who were brother and sister, and sprang from the same father, having a common nature, and being united also in the love of philosophy and art, both obtained as their common portion this land, which was naturally adapted for wisdom and virtue; and there they implanted brave children of the soil, and put into their minds the order of government; their names are preserved, but their actions have disappeared by reason of the destruction of those who received the tradition, and the lapse of ages. For when there were any survivors, as I have already said, they were men who dwelt in the mountains; and they were ignorant of the art of writing, and had heard only the names of the chiefs of the land, but very little about their actions. The names they were willing enough to give to their children; but the virtues and the laws of their predecessors, they knew only by obscure traditions;

and as they themselves and their children lacked for many generations the necessaries of life, they directed their attention to the supply of their wants, and of them they conversed, to the neglect of events that had happened in times long past; for mythology and the enquiry into antiquity are first introduced into cities when they begin to have leisure, and when they see that the necessaries of life have already been provided, but not before.

And this is the reason why the names of the ancients have been preserved to us and not their actions. This I infer because Solon said that the priests in their narrative of that war mentioned most of the names which are recorded prior to the time of Theseus, such as Cecrops, and Erechtheus, and Erichthonius, and Erysichthon, and the names of the women in like manner. Moreover, since military pursuits were then common to men and women, the men of those days in accordance with the custom of the time set up a figure and image of the goddess in full armour, to be a testimony that all animals which associate together, male as well as female, may, if they please, practise in common the virtue which belongs to them without distinction of sex.

Now the country was inhabited in those days by various classes of citizens—there were artisans, and there were husbandmen, and there was also a warrior class originally set apart by divine men. The latter dwelt by themselves, and had all things suitable for nurture and education; neither had any of them anything of their own, but they regarded all that they had as common property; nor did they claim to receive of the other citizens anything more than their necessary food. And they practised all the pursuits which we yesterday described as those of our imaginary guardians.

Concerning the country, the Egyptian priests said what is not only probable but manifestly true, that the boundaries were in those days fixed by the Isthmus, and that in the direction of the continent they extended as far as the heights of Cithaeron and Parnes; the boundary line came down in the direction of the sea, having the district of Oropus on the right, and with the river Asopus as the limit on the left. The land was the best in the world, and was therefore able in those days to support a vast army, raised from the surrounding people. Even the remnant of Attica which now exists may compare with any region in the world for the variety and excellence of its fruits and the suitableness of its pastures to every sort of animal, which proves what I am saying; but in those days the country was fair as now and yielded far more abundant produce.

How shall I establish my words? And what part of it can be truly called a remnant of the land that then was? The whole country is only a long promontory extending far into the sea away from the rest of the continent, while the surrounding basin of the sea is everywhere deep in the neighbourhood of the shore. Many great deluges have taken place during the nine thousand years, for that is the number of years which have elapsed since the time of which I am speaking; and during all this time and through so many changes, there has never been any considerable accumulation of the soil coming down from the mountains, as in other places, but the earth has fallen away all round and sunk out of sight. The consequence is, that in comparison of what then was, there are remaining only the bones of the wasted body, as they may be called, as in the case of small islands, all the richer and softer parts of the soil having fallen away, and the mere skeleton of the land being left.

But in the primitive state of the country, its mountains were high hills covered with soil, and the plains, as they are termed by us, of Phelleus were full of rich earth, and there was abundance of wood in the mountains. Of this last the traces still remain, for although some of the mountains now only afford sustenance to bees, not so very long ago there were still to be seen roofs of timber cut from trees growing there, which were of a size sufficient to cover the largest houses; and there were many other high trees, cultivated by man and bearing abundance of food for cattle. Moreover, the land reaped the benefit of the annual rainfall, not as now losing the water which flows off the bare earth into the sea, but, having an abundant supply in all places, and receiving it into herself and treasuring it up in the close clay soil, it let off into the hollows the streams which it absorbed from the heights, providing everywhere abundant fountains and rivers, of which there may still be observed sacred memorials in places where fountains once existed; and this proves the truth of what I am saying.

Such was the natural state of the country, which was cultivated, as we may well believe, by true husbandmen, who made husbandry their business, and were lovers of honour, and of a noble nature, and had a soil the best in the world, and abundance of water, and in the heaven above an excellently attempered climate.

Now the city in those days was arranged on this wise. In the first place the Acropolis was not as now. For the fact is that a single night of excessive rain washed away the earth and laid bare the rock; at the same time there were earthquakes, and then occurred the extraordinary inundation, which was the third before the great destruction of Deucalion. But in primitive times the hill of the Acropolis extended to the Eridanus and Ilissus, and included the Pnyx on one side, and the Lycabettus as a boundary on the opposite side to the Pnyx, and was all well covered with soil, and level at the top, except in one or two places.

Outside the Acropolis and under the sides of the hill there dwelt artisans, and such of the husbandmen as were tilling the ground near; the warrior class dwelt by themselves around the temples of Athene and Hephaestus at the summit, which moreover they had enclosed with a single fence like the garden of a single house. On the north side they had dwellings in common and had erected halls for dining in winter, and had all the buildings which they needed for their common life, besides temples, but there was no adorning of them with gold and silver, for they made no use of these for any purpose; they took a middle course between meanness and ostentation, and built modest houses in which they and their children's children grew old, and they handed them down to others who were like themselves, always the same. But in summertime they left their gardens and gymnasia and dining halls, and then the southern side of the hill was made use of by them for the same purpose. Where the Acropolis now is, there was a fountain, which was choked by the earthquake, and has left only the few small streams which still exist in the vicinity; but in those days the fountain gave an abundant supply of water for all and of suitable temperature in summer and in winter. This is how they dwelt, being the guardians of their own citizens and the leaders of the Hellenes, who were their willing followers. And they took care to preserve the same number of men and women through all time, being so many as were required for warlike purposes, then as now—that is to say, about twenty thousand.

Such were the ancient Athenians, and after this manner they righteously administered their own land and the rest of Hellas; they were renowned all over Europe and Asia for the beauty of their persons and for the many virtues of their souls, and of all men who lived in those days they were the most illustrious. And next, if I have not forgotten what I heard when I was a child, I will impart to you the character and origin of their adversaries. For friends should not keep their stories to themselves, but have them in common.

Yet, before proceeding further in the narrative, I ought to warn you, that you must not be surprised if you should perhaps hear Hellenic names given to foreigners. I will tell you the reason of this: Solon, who was intending to use the tale for his poem, enquired into the meaning of the names, and found that the early Egyptians in writing them down had translated them into their own language, and he recovered the meaning of the several names and, when copying them out, again translated them, into our language. My great-grandfather, Dropides, had the original writing, which is still in my possession and was carefully studied by me when I was a child. Therefore if you hear names such as are used in this country, you must not be surprised, for I have told how they came to be introduced. The tale, which was of great length, began as follows:

I have before remarked in speaking of the allotments of the gods, that they distributed the whole earth into portions differing in extent, and made for themselves temples and instituted sacrifices. And Poseidon, receiving for his lot the island of Atlantis, begat children by a mortal woman, and settled them in a part of the island, which I will describe.

Looking towards the sea, but in the centre of the whole island, there was a plain which is said to have been the fairest of all plains and very fertile. Near the plain again, and also in the centre of the island at a distance of about fifty stadia, there was a mountain not very high on any side. In this mountain there dwelt one of the earthborn primeval men of that country, whose name was Evenor, and he had a wife named Leucippe, and they had an only daughter who was called Cleito. The maiden had already reached womanhood, when her father and mother died; Poseidon fell in love with her and had intercourse with her, and breaking the ground, inclosed the hill in which she dwelt all round, making alternate zones of sea and land larger and smaller, encircling one another; there were two of land and three of water, which he turned as with a lathe, each having its circumference equidistant every way from the centre, so that no man could get to the island, for ships and voyages were not as yet. He himself, being a god, found no difficulty in making special arrangements for the centre island, bringing up two springs of water from beneath the earth, one of warm water and the other of cold, and making every variety of food to spring up abundantly from the soil.

He also begat and brought up five pairs of twin male children; and dividing the island of Atlantis into ten portions, he gave to the firstborn of the eldest pair his mother's dwelling and the surrounding allotment, which was the largest and best, and made him king over the rest; the others he made princes, and gave them rule over many men, and a large territory. And he named them all; the eldest, who was the first king, he named Atlas, and after him the whole island and the ocean were called Atlantic. To his twin brother, who was born after him, and obtained as his lot the extremity of the island towards the pillars of Heracles, facing the country which is now called the region of Gades in that part of the world, he gave the name which in the Hellenic language is Eumelus, in the language of the country which is named after him, Gadeirus. Of the second pair of twins he called one Ampheres, and the other Evaemon. To the elder of the third pair of twins he gave the name Mneseus, and Autochthon to the one who followed him. Of the fourth pair of twins he called the elder Elasippus, and the younger Mestor. And of the fifth pair he gave to the elder the name of Azaes, and to the younger that of Diaprepes. All these and their descendants for many generations were the inhabitants and rulers of divers islands in the open sea; and also, as has been already said, they held sway in our direction over the country within the pillars as far as Egypt and Tyrrhenia.

Now Atlas had a numerous and honourable family, and they retained the kingdom, the eldest son handing it on to his eldest for many generations; and they had such an amount of wealth as was never before possessed by kings and potentates, and is not likely ever to be again, and they were furnished with everything which they needed, both in the city and the country. For because of the greatness of their empire many things were brought to them from foreign countries, and the island itself provided most of what was required by them for the uses of life.

In the first place, they dug out of the earth whatever was to be found there, solid as well as fusile, and that which is now only a name and was then something more than a name—orichalcum—was dug out of the earth in many parts of the island, being more precious in those days than anything except gold. There was an abundance of wood for carpenter's work, and sufficient maintenance for tame and wild animals. Moreover, there were a great number of elephants in the island; for as there was provision for all other sorts of animals, both for those which live in lakes and marshes and rivers, and also for those which live in mountains and on plains, so was there for the animal which is the largest and most voracious of all.

Also whatever fragrant things there now are in the earth, whether roots, or herbage, or woods, or essences which distil from fruit and flower, grew and thrived in that land; also the fruit which admits of cultivation, both the dry sort, which is given us for nourishment and any other which we use for food—we call them all by the common name of pulse—and the fruits having a hard rind, affording drinks and meats and ointments, and good store of chestnuts and the like, which furnish pleasure and amusement, and are fruits which spoil with keeping, and the pleasant kinds of dessert, with which we console ourselves after dinner, when we are tired of eating—all these that sacred island which then beheld the light of the sun, brought forth fair and wondrous and in infinite abundance.

With such blessings the earth freely furnished them; meanwhile they went on constructing their temples and palaces and harbours and docks. And they arranged the whole country in the following manner: First of all they bridged over the zones of sea which surrounded the ancient metropolis, making a road to and from the royal palace. And at the very beginning they built the palace in the habitation of the god and of their ancestors, which they continued to ornament in successive generations, every king surpassing the one who went before him to the utmost of his power, until they made the building a marvel to behold for size and for beauty. And beginning from the sea they bored a canal of three hundred feet in width and one hundred feet in depth and fifty stadia in length, which they carried through to the outermost zone, making a passage from the sea up to this, which became a harbour, and leaving an opening sufficient to enable the largest vessels to find ingress. Moreover, they divided at the bridges the zones of land which parted the zones of sea, leaving room for a single trireme to pass out of one zone into another, and they covered over the channels so as to leave a way underneath for the ships; for the banks were raised considerably above the water.

Now the largest of the zones into which a passage was cut from the sea was three stadia in breadth, and the zone of land which came next of equal breadth; but the next two zones, the one of water, the other of land, were two stadia, and the one which surrounded the central island was a stadium only in width. The island in which the palace was situated had a diameter of five stadia. All this including the zones and the bridge, which was the sixth part of a stadium in width, they surrounded by a stone wall on every side, placing towers and gates on the bridges where the sea passed in. The stone which was used in the work they quarried from underneath the centre island, and from underneath the zones, on the outer as well as the inner side. One kind was white, another black, and a third red, and as they quarried, they at the same time hollowed out double docks, having roofs formed out of the native rock. Some of their buildings were simple, but in others they put together different stones, varying the colour to please the eye, and to be a natural source of delight. The entire circuit of the wall, which went round the outermost zone, they covered with a coating of brass, and the circuit of the next wall they coated with tin, and the third, which encompassed the citadel, flashed with the red light of orichalcum.

The palaces in the interior of the citadel were constructed on this wise: In the centre was a holy temple dedicated to Cleito and Poseidon, which remained inaccessible and was surrounded by an enclosure of gold; this was the spot where the family of the ten princes first saw the light, and thither the people annually brought the fruits of the earth in their season from all the ten portions, to be an offering to each of the ten. Here was Poseidon's own temple which was a stadium in length, and half a stadium in width, and of a proportionate height, having a strange, barbaric appearance. All the outside of the temple, with the exception of the pinnacles, they covered with silver, and the pinnacles with gold. In the interior of the temple the roof was of ivory, curiously wrought everywhere with gold and silver and orichalcum; and all the other parts, the walls and pillars and floor, they coated with orichalcum.

In the temple they placed statues of gold: there was the god himself standing in a chariot—the charioteer of six winged horses—and of such a size that he touched the roof of the building with his head; around him there were a hundred Nereids riding on dolphins, for such was thought to be the number of them by the men of those days. There were also in the interior of the temple other images which had been dedicated by private persons. And around the temple on the outside were placed statues of gold of all the descendants of the ten kings and of their wives, and there were many other great offerings of kings and of private persons, coming both from the city itself and from the foreign cities over which they held sway. There was an altar too, which in size and workmanship corresponded to this magnificence, and the palaces, in like manner, answered to the greatness of the kingdom and the glory of the temple.

In the next place, they had fountains, one of cold and another of hot water, in gracious plenty flowing; and they were wonderfully adapted for use, by reason of the pleasantness and excellence of their waters. They constructed buildings about them and planted suitable trees; also they made cisterns, some open to the heavens, others roofed over, to be used in winter as warm baths; there were the kings' baths, and the baths of private persons, which were kept apart; and there were separate baths for women, and for horses and cattle, and to each of them they gave as much adornment as was suitable. Of the water which ran off they carried some to the grove of Poseidon, where were growing all manner of trees of wonderful height and beauty, owing to the excellence of the soil, while the remainder was conveyed by aqueducts along the bridges to the outer circles; and there were many temples built and dedicated to many gods; also gardens and places of exercise, some for men, and others for horses in both of the two islands formed by the zones; and in the centre of the larger of the two there was set apart a racecourse of a stadium in width, and in length allowed to extend all round the island, for horses to race in. Also there were guardhouses at intervals for the guards, the more trusted of whom were appointed to keep watch in the lesser zone, which was nearer the Acropolis; while the most trusted of all had houses given them within the citadel, near the persons of the kings. The docks were full of triremes and naval stores, and all things were quite ready for use.

Enough of the plan of the royal palace. Leaving the palace and passing out across the three harbours, you came to a wall which began at the sea and went all round—this was everywhere distant fifty stadia from the largest zone or harbour, and enclosed the whole, the ends meeting at the mouth of the channel which led to the sea. The entire area was densely crowded with habitations; and the canal and the largest of the harbours were full of vessels and merchants coming from all parts, who, from their numbers, kept up a multitudinous sound of human voices, and din and clatter of all sorts night and day.

I have described the city and the environs of the ancient palace nearly in the words of Solon, and now I must endeavour to represent to you the nature and arrangement of the rest of the land. The whole country was said by him to be very lofty and precipitous on the side of the sea, but the country immediately about and surrounding the city was a level plain, itself surrounded by mountains which descended towards the sea; it was smooth and even, and of an oblong shape, extending in one direction three thousand stadia, but across the centre inland it was two thousand stadia. This part of the island looked towards the south, and was sheltered from the north. The surrounding mountains were celebrated for their number and size and beauty, far beyond any which still exist, having in them also many wealthy villages of country folk, and rivers, and lakes, and meadows supplying food enough for every animal, wild or tame, and much wood of various sorts, abundant for each and every kind of work.

I will now describe the plain, as it was fashioned by nature and by the labours of many generations of kings through long ages. It was for the most part rectangular and oblong, and where falling out of the straight line followed the circular ditch. The depth, and width, and length of this ditch were incredible, and gave the impression that a work of such extent, in addition to so many others, could never have been artificial. Nevertheless I must say what I was told. It was excavated to the depth of a hundred feet, and its breadth was a stadium everywhere; it was carried round the whole of the plain, and was ten thousand stadia in length. It received the streams which came down from the mountains, and winding round the plain and meeting at the city, was there let off into the sea. Further inland, likewise, straight canals of a hundred feet in width were cut from it through the plain, and again let off into the ditch leading to the sea—these canals were at intervals of a hundred stadia, and by them they brought down the wood from the mountains to the city, and conveyed the fruits of the earth in ships, cutting transverse passages from one canal into another, and to the city. Twice in the year they gathered the fruits of the earth—in winter having the benefit of the rains of heaven, and in summer the water which the land supplied by introducing streams from the canals.

As to the population, each of the lots in the plain had to find a leader for the men who were fit for military service, and the size of a lot was a square of ten stadia each way, and the total number of all the lots was sixty thousand. And of the inhabitants of the mountains and of the rest of the country there was also a vast multitude, which was distributed among the lots and had leaders assigned to them according to their districts and villages. The leader was required to furnish for the war the sixth portion of a war chariot, so as to make up a total of ten thousand chariots; also two horses and riders for them, and a pair of chariot horses without a seat, accompanied by a horseman who could fight on foot carrying a small shield, and having a charioteer who stood behind the man-at-arms to guide the two horses; also, he was bound to furnish two heavy armed soldiers, two archers, two slingers, three stone shooters and three javelin men, who were light-armed, and four sailors to make up the complement of twelve hundred ships. Such was the military order of the royal city—the order of the other nine governments varied, and it would be wearisome to recount their several differences.

As to offices and honours, the following was the arrangement from the first. Each of the ten kings in his own division and in his own city had the absolute control of the citizens, and, in most cases, of the laws, punishing and slaying whomsoever he would.

Now the order of precedence among them and their mutual relations were regulated by the commands of Poseidon which the law had handed down. These were inscribed by the first kings on a pillar of orichalcum, which was situated in the middle of the island, at the temple of Poseidon, whither the kings were gathered together every fifth and every sixth year alternately, thus giving equal honour to the odd and to the even number. And when they were gathered together they consulted about their common interests, and enquired if anyone had transgressed in anything, and passed judgment, and before they passed judgment they gave their pledges to one another on this wise: There were bulls who had the range of the temple of Poseidon; and the ten kings, being left alone in the temple, after they had offered prayers to the god that they might capture the victim which was acceptable to him, hunted the bulls, without weapons, but with staves and nooses; and the bull which they caught they led up to the pillar and cut its throat over the top of it so that the blood fell upon the sacred inscription.

Now on the pillar, besides the laws, there was inscribed an oath invoking mighty curses on the disobedient. When therefore, after slaying the bull in the accustomed manner, they had burnt its limbs, they filled a bowl of wine and cast in a clot of blood for each of them; the rest of the victim they put in the fire, after having purified the column all round. Then they drew from the bowl in golden cups, and pouring a libation on the fire, they swore that they would judge according to the laws on the pillar, and would punish him who in any point had already transgressed them, and that for the future they would not, if they could help it, offend against the writing on the pillar, and would neither command others, nor obey any ruler who commanded them, to act otherwise than according to the laws of their father Poseidon.

This was the prayer which each of them offered up for himself and for his descendants, at the same time drinking and dedicating the cup out of which he drank in the temple of the god; and after they had supped and satisfied their needs, when darkness came on, and the fire about the sacrifice was cool, all of them put on most beautiful azure robes, and, sitting on the ground, at night, over the embers of the sacrifices by which they had sworn, and extinguishing all the fire about the temple, they received and gave judgment, if any of them had an accusation to bring against anyone; and when they had given judgment, at daybreak they wrote down their sentences on a golden tablet, and dedicated it together with their robes to be a memorial.

There were many special laws affecting the several kings inscribed about the temples, but the most important was the following: They were not to take up arms against one another, and they were all to come to the rescue if anyone in any of their cities attempted to overthrow the royal house; like their ancestors, they were to deliberate in common about war and other matters, giving the supremacy to the descendants of Atlas. And the king was not to have the power of life and death over any of his kinsmen unless he had the assent of the majority of the ten.

Such was the vast power which the god settled in the lost island of Atlantis; and this he afterwards directed against our land for the following reasons, as tradition tells: For many generations, as long as the divine nature lasted in them, they were obedient to the laws, and well-affectioned towards the god, whose seed they were; for they possessed true and in every way great spirits, uniting gentleness with wisdom in the various chances of life, and in their intercourse with one another. They despised everything but virtue, caring little for their present state of life, and thinking lightly of the possession of gold and other property, which seemed only a burden to them; neither were they intoxicated by luxury; nor did wealth deprive them of their self-control; but they were sober, and saw clearly that all these goods are increased by virtue and friendship with one another, whereas by too great regard and respect for them, they are lost and friendship with them.

By such reflections and by the continuance in them of a divine nature, the qualities which we have described grew and increased among them; but when the divine portion began to fade away, and became diluted too often and too much with the mortal admixture, and the human nature got the upper hand, they then, being unable to bear their fortune, behaved unseemly, and to him who had an eye to see, grew visibly debased, for they were losing the fairest of their precious gifts; but to those who had no eye to see the true happiness, they appeared glorious and blessed at the very time when they were full of avarice and unrighteous power.

Zeus, the god of gods, who rules according to law, and is able to see into such things, perceiving that an honourable race was in a woeful plight, and wanting to inflict punishment on them, that they might be chastened and improve, collected all the gods into their most holy habitation, which, being placed in the centre of the world, beholds all created things. And when he had called them together, he spake as follows:

Here ends Plato's unfinished manuscript.

Recommended Reading

Timaeus and Critias, by Plato, translated by Desmond Lee, Penguin, London, 1977. Another, more recent translation of the dialogues in which Atlantis appears, with annotations and an appended note on Atlantis.

Lost Continents: The Atlantis Theme in History, Science, and Literature, by L. Sprague de Camp, Dover, New York, 1970. A detailed survey of the Atlantis idea, its history, and arguments for and against the continent's existence.

Atlantis: The Antediluvian World, by Ignatius Donnelly, Dover, New York, 1976. A reprint of the 1882 book that most popularized the Atlantis myth and that provided arguments still repeated today. The introduction by E. F. Bleiler provides critical, historical perspective.

www.ingramcontent.com/pod-product-compliance
Lightning Source LLC
Chambersburg PA
CBHW032216040426
42449CB00005B/617